The Art Journey

EMELY SOFIA

Copyright © 2020 by Emely Sofia.

ISBN   978-1-970160-88-8 Ebook
ISBN   978-1-970160-89-5 Paperback

All rights reserved. No part of this publication may be reproduced, distributed, or transmitted in any form or by any means, including photocopying, recording, or other electronic or mechanical methods without the prior written permission of the publisher. For permission requests, solicit the publisher via the address below through mail or email with the subject line "Attention: Publication Permission".

The EC Publishing LLC books may be ordered
through booksellers or by contacting:

EC Publishing LLC
116 South Magnolia Ave.
Suite 3, Unit F
Ocala, FL 34471, USA
Direct Line: +1 (352) 644-6538
Fax: +1 (800) 483-1813
http://www.ecpublishingllc.com/

Ordering Information:
Quantity sales. Special discounts are available on quantity purchases by corporations, associations, and others. For details, contact the publisher at the address above.

Printed in the United States of America

Contents

Glowing Light 1
Need Clues! 3
Wait, What? 6
Sorry, Francis! 10
Detention 14
The Night with Rainbow 21
The Gray Out 25
How did you do that? 30
The Big Reveal 33

Glowing Light

"Heads Up! Or should I say heads down." Alexandra Roberts shouted. It was courtyard time in New York's best middle school, and Alex and her friend were playing dodge ball. "Hey, no fair 8 to 5!" called her friend Francis Brown. Alex took the ball and threw it at Francis. Before it hit him, the school bell rang. "Ha, ha! You didn't get me." Francis teased. After school Alex and Francis were going on a walk to the park. "Hey Alex", Francis said. "Yeah?" replied Alex. "What's that?" Francis continued. "What's-wow!" Alex said looking at a strange glowing light.

"Let's go see what it is!" Francis cried, running toward the trees. "Wait for me!" Alex shouted. "Hey, the glowing light turned off." She said, when she caught up with Francis. "Yeah, where'd it go?" said Francis. Suddenly, it lit up again. "Hey, it's back." Alex said, running towards it again. "Alex, time to go!" called a voice. "Francis, come on!!!!" said a second voice.

At Alex's home, Alex was doing homework, and just then, her notepad turned gray! "Mom! Dad! My notepad turned gray!" Alex shouted. "Tell me about it, look at the dishes!" Alex's mom said pointing at the sink.

"Why is everything gray?" Alex asked Francis at the skate park. Francis hopped on his skateboard and shrugged "I don't know. Everything's turning gray and bland," he said. Alex clipped her helmet on and hopped on her skateboard. "Maybe someone is painting everything." Alex said. Francis shook his head. "Hey, its' the strange glowing light!"

Need Clues!

"Okay, if you were a painter, where would you paint?" Alex asked, pulling out her notebook. "Uh, the wall near the car wash." Francis replied, taking paints from out of his backpack. Alex opened her notebook and wrote: *1. Near the car wash.* She looked up and said, "let's see if the wall near the car wash is gray. Um, schedule it tomorrow at 3:30." Francis walked to Alex's bedroom window and looked outside. The glowing light lit up so brightly, and then it turned off. "Maybe the light has something to do with it," he said. "Maybe when it turns on something turns gray!" Alex added. Francis nodded. "Perfect! We're back on track!"

The next day, Alex went over to Francis' house. It was Saturday, so they could be together all day. "Good morning Alex. Come into my room." Francis said, leading Alex through his house. "Ha ha! I have the best idea EVER!" Francis said, showing Alex a large chalkboard. The chalkboard had a math problem on the top that was crossed out. Then there was a picture of three things. One was Alex and Francis behind the wall. Another, were lame-looking trees, and the last one was Alex and Francis dancing. "Tada! Okay, here's the plan. We check if the wall near the car wash is gray.

Then, we check the glowing light, then --- " Francis' speech got interrupted by his mom. "Francis, we have to go shopping!"

"Okay!" Francis called. "Sorry, Alex. Maybe another time." Alex sighed. "Hey, maybe I can do that plan," she said to herself. She ran out of Francis' house and ran to hers. "Alex, is that you!" called Alex's dad. "Uh, yes! I'm going to the park!" Alex called. She ran upstairs and grabbed her bookbag. She threw her library books all over her room, and then she grabbed her gray notepad and a pen with cats all over it. "Alex, come home in an hour, okay? We have shopping to do." Alex's mom asked. "Sure, okay." Alex said quickly. Then she ran outside and rode her bike to the car wash.

THE ART JOURNEY

When she arrived, rain started pouring out of the sky. Alex's bike had a built-in umbrella so it popped out when you push a button. "Hey, Alex!" called a familiar voice. It was Francis. His car was driving towards the store. Alex waved as the car drove out of sight. Then she rode her bike to the wall near the car wash. It was gray. Suddenly, the strange glowing light lit up again! When it turned off, Alex's bike suddenly turned gray --- and bland.

Thirty minutes later, it stopped raining. Alex ran toward the trees. As she ran, flowers beside her started turning gray. Finally, she reached the end. Something was sparkling in front of her. The sparkles were covering whatever it was, but a moment later, it showed. It was a portal! "Wow!" Alex said in surprise. She stepped right in. "Hello and welcome. I am Rainbow Stream" a voice said.

Wait, What?

Alex was in awe. "What is your name?" the voice asked politely. "uh-A-Alexandra R-Roberts." Alex started. She took a deep breath. "Every one calls me Alex. W-where are you?" she continued. A human-sized fairy came towards Alex. "What's your name again?" Alex asked. "Rainbow Stream. It is nice to meet you Alexandra," the fairy said. "I will give you a tour if you would like." Alex shook her head slowly. Then she felt a voice inside of her saying, "yes!" so, then she nodded.

Rainbow Stream smiled and said, "everybody calls me Rainbow." Alex suddenly remembered something important! "Oh, my goodness! I forgot about mom! a-and shopping! Sorry Rainbow, I have to leave. I'll see you, uh, maybe tomorrow after school!" she said. Rainbow nodded and floated away.

"Alexandra Roberts! Where have you been?!" Alex's mom asked when she got home. Alex bit her lip. "I um, found this portal thingy, and, ahh, saw a human-sized fairy, and um, her name is Rainbow Stream," she said slowly. Her mom stared at her. "Well, go visit human-sized stream of rainbows fairy later, as in never! And stay when it is time to shop!" she yelled. Alex was about to shout out, *It's Rainbow Stream!* But she refused, all that came out was, "Mom, I'm sorry. Tomorrow I'll stay at school extra! and---"

she paused. She remembered what she told Rainbow, after school she'd visit her. Alex's dad grabbed a plastic bag and said, "shopping time!" Alex sighed. She went to change her wet clothes into nice clothes. The glowing light shone brighter than ever! Alex heard a loud scream from next door. She immediately peeked out of her window and noticed her neighbor was gray! "Wow! I have to stop whatever is going on," she said. Suddenly, Alex heard another loud scream! It was from her mom. Yep, Mrs. Roberts was gray. "Uhh, mom, I changed, you okay?" she asked, trying not to think about Rainbow. "Don't worry, I'll go shopping with Alex and you can stay here." Mr. Roberts said. "yeah, you should definitely go without me." Mrs. Roberts replied.

In the car, Alex and her Dad had a little conversation. "Alex, what were you actually doing in that hour your mom gave you? Mr. Roberts asked. "Dad, I actually met Rainbow Stream! I went into the woods and found a magic portal! Believe me! Please!" Alex said.

Mr. Roberts still didn't believe Alex.

At the store, Alex pushed the shopping cart while Mr. Roberts bought the items. It started raining again. "Dad, can I get that planner?" Alex asked, pointing at a small planner. Mr. Roberts thought for a moment. "Hey, isn't that Francis?" he asked. Alex had to think fast! If Francis knew that Alex did his plan without him, she would be in big trouble. "You can have the planner, Alex." Mr. Roberts said. Alex grabbed the planner from the shelf and ran to a different aisle. She hid from Francis, but tried to make sure her dad could still see her. "Dad!" she whispered. "Dad, come here." Mr. Robert rushed toward Alex. "Alex, we have to leave." he said. Francis appeared in front of Alex. "Hi Alex, what's wrong?" he asked.

Sorry, Francis!

"I might have done your plan, like, without you." Alex said to Francis in the car. "Alex! Why? I thought friends do things together. You know what that means!" Francis said turning to Mr. Roberts. "Mr. Roberts," he said politely, "can you drop me off at my house?"

Mr. Roberts turned to Francis' house driveway. "Wait, Francis, I'm sorry!" Alex cried. Francis ignored Alex.

Alex went home after that. She just lost a friend. Maybe she could get all her friends back. Like, Bella, Joseph, Mary, and maybe even Francis. Alex decided to write a letter to each one of her old friends, including Francis. Hopefully, they get encouraged.

"Mom, I need you to put these letters in the mailbox. And dad, can you please invite Francis over for some snacks?" Alex said to her parents. Both parents did what they were assigned to do.

"Thank you, Mr. Roberts, but I'm not hungry." Francis said. Later, Alex went to the park again. She went deep into the woods and went into the portal, again. "Rainbow! Rainbow Stream!" she shouted. Her friend didn't show up, so she decided to explore. She walked around, looking at displays of art. "Alex, there you are. I have been looking everywhere for you." Rainbow said flying toward her. "Rainbow! I need your help." Alex said. "I lost a friend. His name is Francis. Please help me get him back." Alex explained. Suddenly, Alex remembered something. "Rainbow, do you know why everything is turning gray?" she asked. "Oh Alex, do you see our clouds? They are gray. It will turn gray and bland if we do not fix it." Rainbow replied. "Oh, I can help you with the clouds if you can help me with Francis." Alex said. Rainbow nodded. "Go to the human world, you will have your problem solved." She said.

The next day, Alex woke up and got ready for school. She got right on the bus. At school, Alex took her books out of her locker. Francis was behind her. "Alex, meet me after school, please," he said.

After school, Alex met up with Francis. "Francis, I am so sorry. I miss you." Alex said. "I miss you too." Francis said. "Friends?" Alex asked. "Friends." Francis replied. "I love you." Alex said. Then, they hugged.

Detention

After Alex and Francis reunited, they went to the park. "Come here, across the woods. Trust me; there is a surprise at the end," Alex said. They went across the woods and found the portal. "Wow!" Francis said. "Did I fix the correct Francis?" Rainbow asked. Alex nodded. "And here he is now," she said. "Hello. I'm Francis Brown." Francis said sticking his hand out. "And you must be Rainbow Stream," he added. Rainbow nodded. "Oh, uh, Francis, the reason everything is turning gray is that those clouds up there are making stuff gray," Alex said.

Alex, Francis, and Rainbow all went behind the wall. "Who would like to swim?" Rainbow asked pointing at a paint pool. She took off her boots. Francis threw his boots and dived in. "What is wrong, Alex?" Rainbow asked. Alex dipped her hand into the water and said, "I can't see without my glasses. Plus, I don't like swimming."

THE ART JOURNEY

The next thing they did was look at Rainbow's art. Alex got bored while Francis clapped and cheered. "Alex, I am sure you will like the last activity," Rainbow said.

"Presenting, the flying Art Dinos!" Alex gasped in fear. "Dinos!? I thought they were extinct!" she said. Francis hopped on a Dino. "weeee!" he yelled. Alex sighed. "Rainbow, I didn't like anything!" she said. "Alex, there is a special activity just for you," Rainbow said. Alex smiled as she saw a purple sunset – and the clouds were not purple. The sun was!

The next day, Alex and Francis went to the park. They completely skipped school! After school, they decided to take their books home to work on school work. Of course, the teacher had caught them.

"You two shouldn't have skipped school!" the teacher yelled. She took them both to the classroom. Then, she sat them down. "I'm going to tell your parents, and guess what! DETENTION for you two! On Saturday!"

"So, I need you to help with our detention problem." Alex explained to Rainbow about detention later in the day. "I am sorry but I cannot fix that problem. But I do have a plan," Rainbow said.

The next day was Saturday and like the teacher had said, detention on Saturday.

"I will shrink and act like a normal fairy. No one will see me," Rainbow explained to Francis and Alex outside. Rainbow went to the real world with Francis and Alex to make sure they had the best detention ever. "Rainbow, shrink now!" Francis whispered to Rainbow. Rainbow shrank and hid in Alex's hair.

"Hello everybody, and welcome to detention! Math homework nobody did is first! What two numbers would you add to get 888?" said the teacher.

"I'm so bored," Alex whispered to Francis. "I know. I am too," Francis whispered back. Rainbow popped her head out of Alex's hair. "I will fix that Alex and Francis," she said in Alex's ear. She grabbed Alex's paintbrush and started painting a picture. Rainbow swoosh the paintbrush around the paper. "What's the drawing?" Francis whispered. Alex shrugged. Rainbow's painting seemed to be a picture of Alex. Francis and Alex giggled. "Francis, Alex, do you two want to be separated?" The teacher interrupted.

"No," Alex said picking Rainbow up. "We'd like to stay together." "As I was saying, you take away the e from here. Then, add the e," the teacher explained. "Rainbow, me and Alex are having a sleepover. Want to come?" Francis said. "I guess so. I have other friends waiting, but I will tell them where I am going."

Later (about 30 minutes later), the detention class ended. "Glad that's over," Alex said putting her books in the locker. "I know, right. That was BORING! I almost fell asleep," Francis said. Alex nodded and giggled. "Let's get outside. Rainbow's got to change to her normal size," she said. Francis and Alex ran outside while Rainbow flew behind them. They scampered behind the large tree. Rainbow got back into her normal size. "I will see you at bedtime," she said flying out of sight.

The Night with Rainbow

That night, Rainbow was a little late. "Hi Francis, what did you bring?" Alex said, when Francis arrived. "My video games. Where's Rainbow?" Francis replied. Alex shrugged. "She's not here yet. Maybe her friends invited her to a different sleepover," she said. Francis put his video games down. "Hey, isn't that Rainbow?" he said, waving. "Hello Francis and Alex," said Rainbow. "I'll be right back. I'm getting another bowl of popcorn," said Francis.

He walked out of the room. Alex turned around. "Rainbow, how do you sleep in that portal? Do you have blankets and pillows like us?" she asked. "There are blankets. They are called Rainbow blankets," Rainbow replied. "But your name is Rainbow," Alex said, confused. "I am Rainbow but that is what they call it," said Rainbow. "I'm back! Here is some more popcorn," Francis interrupted. "Okay, Francis. May I have some?" Rainbow asked. "Sure, you are like, the guest of honor," said Francis. Then he turned on a loud video game. A little human bounced around the screen. It was more of a peg. Francis pushed buttons for it to move. The peg bounced over to a star.

"Rainbow, do you want to try?" Francis asked, giving Rainbow the remote controls. "Okay, but how do you play?" Rainbow asked. "Oh, it's easy! Push that to go left and that to go right. And that button to jump," Francis replied, pointing at different controls. Alex set up two sleeping bags. "Rainbow, did you bring any rainbow blankets?" asked Alex. "Yes, I will set my bed up later," Rainbow replied. She started playing the video game the way Francis told her. Francis took a popcorn bowl.

"After this, we can watch movies. I'll make a list of some we can watch," said Alex. She started writing, Tinkerbell, Frozen, and The Little Mermaid. Rainbow peeked at the list. "I love these movies – all of them," she said. Francis peeked at the list. "That's all girly stuff! It should be more like this!" he said, taking the paper and pencil.

Then he wrote, The Lion King, Hercules and The Emperor's New Groove. He handed the list to Alex. "All of this stuff is boring," said Alex. Francis looked at his watch. "We have exactly one hour until our bedtime," he said. Rainbow flew over to Alex's bed. "Pillow fight!' she yelled, throwing a pillow at Alex. Alex picked up the pillow and threw it at Francis. Then Francis grabbed it and threw it at Rainbow. Alex took two more pillows. "Double attack!" she yelled throwing them at Francis. One he dodged, while the other hit him. The one he dodged hit Rainbow. One hour later, everybody went to sleep. Rainbow set out her rainbow blankets and said, "good night."

The Gray Out

"Francis, let's go see Rainbow!" Alex called running through the woods. "Whoa! Why is the portal gray?" she said. "It's not. The inside of the portal is gray," Francis replied. They hopped into the portal. Big dark gray clouds covered the sky in the portal. Rainbow came falling from the sky all gray! "Alexandra, Francis, the dark clouds are turning everything gray. I need your help!" Francis' jaw dropped. "Why are you gray, Rainbow?" he asked. "I tried to stop the clouds but I turned gray," Rainbow replied. "You two need shelter like that," she said, pointing at a small shelter.

The three ran out of the portal. "Rainbow, will the clouds go out of the portal and into the human world?" Francis asked, watching the clouds come towards the exit of the portal. "Yes. They will," Rainbow said. One moment later, the clouds came to the human world! "Alex! There you are," Mrs. Roberts said.

"Mom, you said you don't want to go out in public all gray!" Alex said. Mrs. Roberts shrugged. "I was worried about you," she said, opening her umbrella. Gray rain puddles were everywhere. Later, Alex was at home. She watched the gray rain turn things gray. "Alex, Francis is here. He said he has to talk to you," Mr. Roberts said, with Francis following behind him. Mr. Roberts walked out of the room.

"Alex, Rainbow is in your house somewhere. She told me. And by the way, Rainbow shrank," Francis said. Alex pulled the covers off of her bed. And there was a small gray fairy. It was Rainbow.

"Francis, thank you for telling Alex about this," Rainbow said, floating towards Alex. Then she grew back into her normal size.

Alex led them to a chalkboard. "Here's my plan. The clouds are gray and bland, and last week in the science fair I won second place with my clouds that rain. If the clouds are gray and bland, we can add colors to it!" she explained, pointing everything out. Then she grabbed a bottle with her clouds in it. She added a bit of food coloring, and the clouds turned red! She made the clouds rain, and it was red rain! "Wow! That is amazing!" Rainbow said.

Alex and Francis snuck outside with Rainbow. Alex gave Rainbow a raincoat. Rainbow used magic to make special paint that will turn everything into its normal color. Rainbow took a paint can and flew up to the clouds. Suddenly, Rainbow felt a shock! It was gray lighting that hit her wings!

How did you do that?

Rainbow's wings were all bent and were breaking! Alex and Francis caught her in time. They went to Alex's house.

"I brought you a snack," Francis said, taking a tray to Rainbow. Alex sighed. "Can you use magic to fix your wings?" she asked. "Alex, I get my magic from my wings," Rainbow said carefully tapping on her wings. She looked outside of the window. "Alex, Francis, I have a great idea! I made the paint and I still have it! And whoever touches my wings while they are broken, will have my magic! Well, except for the wings. You can use magic to make the paint float to the sky! Then fix my wings. But you will not have the powers anymore," she explained.

Alex touched her wings. She moved paint up into the sky and it worked! "Mom, dad, go outside!" she called. They went outside and Mrs. Roberts was her normal color again. "Alex," called a voice. It was Mary! One of Alex's old friends. Alex got two friends back. "Fairy! It's Rainbow Stream!" Mr. Roberts exclaimed.

The Big Reveal

The next day was show-and-tell-one-friend at school. Alex and Francis were buddied-up to tell a special speech about a friend.

"Our friend is special. She doesn't live in New York. She lives in a magic art portal. You might not believe us, but we have proof," they said together. Rainbow came to the school and floated above everybody. "Thank you, Alexandra Roberts," she said. "And you too Francis Brown."

The whole class was amazed and cheered.

THE END

www.ingramcontent.com/pod-product-compliance
Lightning Source LLC
Chambersburg PA
CBHW041218070526
44583CB00006B/172